The Cariboo Horses

MCCLELLAND AND STEWART LIMITED / TORONTO / MONTREAL

ALFRED PURDY

The Cariboo Horses

Third printing 1976

© *1965, 1972 by Alfred Purdy*

0-7710-7193-0

ACKNOWLEDGEMENTS

Delta / Evidence / The Canadian Forum / Tamarack Review / Prism Volume 63 / Island / The Bloody Horse / CBC Wednesday Night

The Canadian Publishers
McClelland and Stewart Limited / 25 Hollinger Road / Toronto

Contents

The Cariboo Horses

At 100 Mile House the cowboys ride in rolling
stagey cigarettes with one hand reining
skittish bronco rebels on a morning grey as stone
—so much like riding dangerous women
        with whiskey coloured eyes—
such women as once fell dead with their lovers
with fire in their heads and slippery froth on thighs
—Beaver and Carrier women maybe or
        Blackfoot squaws far past the edge of this valley
on the other side of those two toy mountain ranges
        from the sunfierce plains beyond—

But only horses
        waiting in stables
hitched at taverns
        standing at dawn
pastured outside the town with
jeeps and fords and chevvys and
busy muttering stake trucks rushing
importantly over roads of man's devising
over the safe known roads of the ranchers
families and merchants of the town—
        On the high prairie
are only horse and rider
        wind in dry grass
clopping in silence under the toy mountains
dropping sometimes and
        lost in the dry grass
        golden oranges of dung—

Only horses
                no stopwatch memories or palace ancestors
not Kiangs hauling undressed stone in the Nile Valley
and having stubborn Egyptian tantrums or
Onagers racing thru Hither Asia and
the last Quagga screaming in African highlands
                lost relatives of these
                whose hooves were thunder
the ghosts of horses battering thru the wind
whose names were the wind's common usage
whose life was the sun's
                arriving here at chilly noon
                in the gasoline smell of the
                dust and waiting 15 minutes
                at the grocer's—

Malcolm Lowry

Not much to remember
    going to see the soused writer and
    bursting from dull green wood
    out to the live green water
with introductions and awkward handshakes
on a shore full of driftwood and stones with blue
boats on a blue horizon
not seeming to move but moving anyway and
ourselves unacquainted with one another
unnoticed by the sea
And in the nature of things I shouldn't
have been surprised if there hadn't
been any gin that day
    and getting drunk on tea

Not much reason
to remember that bit of land or
the old iron ship I found later
on an exploring trip I guess
the hectic spots of flame still dance
on the cheeks of the salty old whore
of a city over the water shine
still on a blue or a grey day
and the gulls no doubt still scream
louder than ever in a noisy masquerade
of permanence
             but that red face is dead

Not much reason
        to remember him on the beach
        no knowing even the stones
        he shifted in the exuberant morning
        or what trees have fallen or
if some of the mountains were restless
        and moved
slightly moving also a little down there on the water only
the composition of colours must be
        much the same
And buried in a nest of deep grass a couple
of old gin bottles
        but they're empty

Postscript

I say the stanza ends
      but it never does
there being something continual,
apart from the blaze of man, in a woman—
At least he somehow thinks there is.
After a parting grimly convivial
nostalgia comes like an old shaman,
you travel backward in time and finally
come to a place she never was to
some small town with desolate streets and
yourself inside yourself
      unable to get out or
a city sheerly grey with a child's ennui—
You come to a place she never was and
everything that happened happened
      without her:
tho blindly in darkness
      lovers were coming together
the gilled foetus formed
      the flippered thing
climbing the long climb up from animal
arriving anonymous one calendar morning
come screaming a child-like-woman's tantrum
      onto the white delivery table—

You travel backward in time and come
to the double rorschach bedsheet blot and
the silvery look she had in the bathtub and
the twisting double standard of pain in the guts
of love that was always much less than freedom
                    can never be freedom—
And you come to the power struggle and quarrelling
                    over the deed and title
of whatever shone thru your eyes at each other
                    and you come to the sweating
welded flesh in the bundling bedsheet sea until
                    morning comes
the shivering cold and complicated awakening comes—

(The snail has lost its shell and toothless lion
grumbles alone in dangerous country—
The rhino's horns have fallen along a trail
deep in dark woods crowded with big game hunters—
The eagle has left its claws behind in the clawed sky
the antelopes have all gone lame and
the lover has no luck at all—)

You come to a place she never was
                    or will be in time that circles
around behind and traps you here and now and you
                    weep because you do not weep
                    for each other
                    (or very little)
                    but all young things
the new and continually arriving hardly-able-to-stand thin
                    that live here
in the trees and the woods and the green fields of summer—

The Madwoman on the Train

I've always been going somewhere—Vancouver
or old age or somewhere ever since I can remember:
and this woman leaning over me, this madwoman,
while I was sleeping, whispering, "Do you take drugs?"
And the sight of her yellow-white teeth biting
the dark open wide and white eyes like marbles

children play with but no children play with marbles
like those—saying, "Do you take drugs?" And Vancouver
must be somewhere near this midnight I can't remember
where tho only the sister holding the madwoman,
fighting her: me saying stupidly, "No, no drugs."
She wanting to talk and sitting there biting

at something I couldn't see what the hell she was biting,
only her white eyes like aching terrible marbles
and mouth crying out, "I don't want to go to Vancouver!
Don't let them take me!" She didn't remember
the sad scared children, children of the madwoman
herself, recognized only me the stranger, asking what drugs

I took and wouldn't stop asking that. What such drugs
do besides closing those eyes and keeping those teeth
                                        from biting
that tongue into rags and soothing a forehead damp
                                        as marble's
cold stone couldn't be altogether bad eh? All the way
                                        to Vancouver
where I was going and thought I could remember
having lived once I comforted the madwoman

while the sister minded her frightened children: madwoman,
courtesan, mother, wife, in that order. Such drugs
as I know of don't cause this snapping and biting
at shadows or eyes like glaring lacustral marbles
and mouth crying, "Don't let them take me to Vancouver!"
And leaning her head on my shoulder's scared calm . . .
                                                I remember

now the promise I made and do not wish to remember
going somewhere and falling asleep on the train and
                                    the madwoman
shakes me softly awake again and, "Yes, I do take drugs,"
I say to her and myself. "I get high on hemp and peyote
                                        biting
at scraps of existence I've lost all the smoky limitless
                                        marbles
I found in my life once lost long before Vancouver—"

I've forgotten that child, his frantic scratching and biting
for something he wanted and lost—but it wasn't marbles.
I remember the Mountie waiting, then the conductor's
                    "Vancouver next! Vancouver!"

Thank God I'm Normal

From the west coast X writes,
"—someone at CBC is trying to block me."
In Toronto W says, "I want him to die,
if he'd just die—
Then I'd have enough money to publish my poems."
Only the guy in Montreal says nothing,
having gotten all the awards going already.
Besides, he's so neurotic he's written
a handy literary guide to the bughouse.
From Calgary, "They won't publish my poems.
They're afraid of em, for I tell the truth.
And They can't stand Truth!"
From the Maritimes: We've got a tradition behind us!
(It's what they sit on.)
Me, I'm like all the rest: I wanta be famous!
But I'm not gonna be paranoic
        I'm not I'm not I'm not I'm not I'm not—
Anyway, I don't know how to end this.
But the morning mail drops in the slot
and a letter from the scholarship people says,
"It is with regret that we inform you—"
    Why—why, the sonsabitches!

Music on a Tombstone

In Roblin's Mills old Owen Roblin
came almost fully awake in his lifetime once
owned 6 houses and built an octagonal one he
slept alone with his woman beside him
beard outside the quilts in zero weather
breath smelling of snoose and apple cider
dreaming not of houris and other men's wives
but his potash works and the sawmill hearing
only the hard tusked music of wheels turning
and hardly ever heard anything soft he
did know one March that June was early
(didst thou then old Owen hear the robins?)
built a gristmill and a village gradually
grew round it and the deep woods vanished and
his wife whelped every nine months eventually
    he died in his sleep age 97
    and everything ended

Note: Owen Roblin was born in 1806, died 1903. He built his gristmill and octagonal house in 1842, and the village of Roblin's Mills (now Ameliasburg) came into being. In 1914 one of old Owen's descendents rented the mill to a man named Taylor from Belleville, and Taylor prospered under this rental agreement. Then Will Roblin demanded a share in the profits. Taylor refused, and walked out. The mill never operated again, and the village declined—

Percy Lawson

(Contract Negotiator—Vancouver Upholsterers' Union)

Sitting with Lawson in 1954
        sitting with Percy Lawson
ill at ease in the boss's panelled office
after work hours talking of nothing
talking of practically almost nothing
a lousy nickel raise that is
        haggling over a lousy nickel
and maybe besides the long and hourly
bearable toil of an almost lifetime
(East Indians: 35 years
        Canadians: 70—figures approximate)
Listen in again in the boss's panelled office
        listen to Lawson
listen to Percy Lawson
—thinking of girls in the cutting room
afraid of the union
        afraid for their jobs and
thinking of me—afraid of Watt or
not afraid
        only wanting to be liked
and knowing for sure I'm not
Thinking of Lawson
        up from the coal mines
on the island and gotten fat
since talking and haggling and
being afraid of practically nothing

but death and his wife and damn near
      everything but not
not bosses
not Watt
And what's the contract news from Watt who
if I said what I thought he was would
sue me for damn near everything
would sue me right now in a poem and
get a judgement for one lying lyric
      I can't write
      (I'll be damned if I write)
in praise of Watt
in praise of
      practically nothing
But I listen to Percy Lawson
      haggling over a lousy nickel
listen to the sonuvabitch
      haggling over a lousy nickel
the twentieth part of a dollar that
      winks among the words
like a clean magician's coin
born from virginal nothing and not
mined or smelted and sweated and laboured for for
the twentieth part of a wasted hour back there
in the silvery guts of a labouring terribly useful lifetime
In a tactical pause between the chop
      of words Lawson turns
the little fat man probably dead now
      turns then and gives
me a gold-toothed grin

Notes on Painting

The early Italians—Giotto, Fra Angelico,
including Botticelli's Venus—
candied myths for children,
or so they seem to me.
And when you think of it,
Sasetta's "Journey of the Magi"
was probably copied by
Ingmar Bergman in "The Seventh Seal":
the castle, mediaeval jester, the night horses,
trudging along the horizon's rim,
seeking refuge from prowling death:
which at the time of the Crusades
could just as easily have been
whooping cough or measles—

But when you come to the 17th century,
Franz Hals and Holbein's family:
I've seen that woman in Ameliasburg,
and her husband like an animal,
living in the killing suburbs
of poverty and ignorance:
they quarrel on the main street once
or twice a week and the village
watches while the husband beats
his wife till someone says:
"Better go inside the house and fight . . ."

El Greco's Cardinal, Nino de Guevara, well
I just don't believe in that face.
As a kid in Trenton tho I remember
the town idiot, old Joe Barr,
about 40, with a week's beard,
his mind made of cloud-candy,
a small town christ minus the miracles,
turning to face the tormenting children:
his face in that instant could have been a cardinal's,
knowing everything life was for him—
But the next instant a slimy silver
dribble ran down his chin,
and the stones fell around him—

Or Velasquez' "Innocent X,"
wise and cunning,
with a piggishness to his nose
popes get before they know
they're gonna be popes and
can't help it—
During the war at Trenton RCAF base
I knew some sergeants could've been popes,
they already had the piggishness and cunning:
a little authority made them monsters,
a lot would've made them saints—
I transplant Bill Botham's head to Innocent's body,
and Parkes and Jackson (the typewriter mechanic),
and Moses O'Leary (the ex-boxer) become
unholy cardinals in red hats roaring
commands on the parade square making
recruits piss their pants and officers
salute by mistake and curse—drinking
beer at the Quinte or Sergeants' Mess with
wise eyes and pig noses and red and
wet in the heat and stinking like generals
rommel and montgomery in the western desert
roaring among the dead men and

Bill Botham's head on the pope's body saying:
"Gentlemen, I am Innocent X! Genuflect, you bastards!"

Or the painted women: Ingres' women maybe
Delacroix's Liberty leading the Grey Cup parade
(what makes the draperies rustle so?
not a man but Coach Sazio)—And
fat women slopping themselves untidily
onto a neat canvas signed in one corner: Rubens—
I've never seen women like those,
for I remember only their voices and not their names and
whether their bodies' white liquids were sweet or sour now
in the singing distant guts of the moment—

And Breughel's "Slaughter of the Innocents"—isn't it strange
how evil is never believable on canvas?
And the Spanish soldiers are having great fun
(like children pulling the wings from flies),
and spear babies and trample women under
the hooves of their horses shouting boyishly:
"Oh, very good, Pedro!" and "Fine stroke, Manuel!"
(suffering bodies topple—and really
the Dutch peasants are so colourful my dear)
Isn't it strange that you search
thru paintings of all the old masters,
and see evil only obliquely:
its results but never the cause
among the sunlit stones
waiting to be identified?
Unless you say mere ruthlessness and cunning are
evil and then you can find it then you
can see it in all those old paintings,
the early Italians and the Dutch Masters,
unfaded in the fading pigments of human love
from Giotto to Picasso, on the street outside the house,
and in
          where you're writing—

Engraved on a Tomb

Off the train and so hungry a
nova sucking pap at the stars' lunch
counter to make rock porridge with would
blush and burp six asteroids to watch the
way I finished a plate of ham and eggs and
                    Home
after 8 weeks away I picked her up
by the elbows and danced her across the
room and said "Honey you're awful lucky
I ever came home you're so bloody homely
and the girls out there so beautiful so
hell it must be love I guess" I said and there
was a fly buzzing up near the ceiling of
the bedroom and nails in the wood
shrieked a little quietly and when we came
outside together later after it had rained
hard enough for the grass to wet our feet and
            she said musingly
                    "You bastard"
                    "Hey?"

Necropsy of Love

If it came about you died
it might be said I loved you:
love is an absolute as death is,
and neither bears false witness to the other—
But you remain alive.

No, I do not love you
                  hate the word,
that private tyranny inside a public sound,
your freedom's yours and not my own:
but hold my separate madness like a sword,
and plunge it in your body all night long.

If death shall strip our bones of all but bones,
then here's the flesh and flesh that's drunken-sweet
as wine cups in deceptive lunar light:
reach up your hand and turn the moonlight off,
and maybe it was never there at all,
so never promise anything to me:
but reach across the darkness with your hand,
reach across the distance of tonight,
and touch the moving moment once again
                  before you fall asleep—

Policeman

Is kindly public servant
winking apples from grocer
lollypopping gold coral
buttons anchoring mediterranean belly
Is heroic idol
shooting it out with dirty tv crooks who
didn't get to Freud or Jung in Grade Six tho
they tried never so hard and
consoling their bereaved and weeping old mommas
Is tyrant of cities
rescuer knight errant blue bully you
barracuda   cruising the dangerous streets
at night issuing terse overheard orders to
householders re late parties & overturned garbage cans
father of three
lodge member
pillar of
respected by
deferred to
Friendly feller
respecter of personages
Is god with a gun
the giant Argus peering into public disloyalty
the Guarde Civile Gestapo Mounties and F.B.I.
master of bludgeon billy and leather truncheon
and brutal beatings and parking tickets and necessary
as hell was this Gabriel this comic flat footed angel
eye globular and faceted in peacock blue night
Is god dammit
and I've got troubles enough god without
(being a man—god)
feeling guilty forever for what I am as it is—

Sunday Swim

In the dazzling water
I waggle both shoulders
as a bird does and
serrated fingertips are
feathers beating the water sky
are wings bursting thru storms
of foam embracing my body
observing its own dream
as the distance from one place
to another in an arc of light a
trick of seeing starting point
and objective together and
they are the same—
Or returning to shallows
lost in reflections
of trees and sky classrooms
behind rumours of movement—
Or beating the silvery climate
with winged glorying shoulders
with hunger that stays hunger
and feeding remains unfed—
Or feeling the body's exaltation
as the first gods must have:
I with the blind folding water's
green jelly against my eyes
sweating and racing among
rainbow tribes of sunfish—
They with their wooden rattles
and stag horn helmets are

Cro-Magnon impressarios flourishing
their bodies' contorted wires
gasping thru snorkel centuries in
drunken oxygen dreams and
mirages of timeless lakes that
terrify all the tribes—
Both of us stopping at once and
searching the sky uneasily for
the sun and the moon's
bright candidate—

Song of the
Impermanent Husband

Oh I would
           I would in a minute
if the cusswords and bitter anger couldn't—
if the either/or quarrel didn't—
and the fat around my middle wasn't—
if I was young if
              I wasn't so damn sure
I couldn't find another maddening bitch
like you holding on for dear life to
all the different parts of me for
twenty or twenty
                thousand years
I'd leave in the night like
a disgraced caviar salesman
               descend the moonlight
stairs to Halifax
     (uh—no—not Halifax)
well then Toronto
         uh
I guess not Toronto either/or
nouveau riche Vancouver down
                     down
                       down
the dark stairs to
the South Seas' sunlit milky reefs and
     the jungle's green
          unending bank account with
all the brown girls being brown
       as they can be and all

the one piece behinds stretched tight tonight
in small sarongs not to be touched tho Oh
beautiful as an angel's ass without the genitals
and me
             in Paris like a smudged Canadian postcard and
(dear me)
          all the importuning white and lily girls
of Rue Pigalle
             and stroll
the sodden London streets and
                find a sullen foggy woman who
enjoyed my odd colonial ways and send
a postcard back to you about my faithfulness and
talk about the lovely lovely English weather
I'd be the slimiest most uxorious wife deserter
                my shrunk amoeba self absurd inside
a saffron girl's geography and
hating me between magnetic nipples
but
    fooling no one in all the sad
    and much emancipated world
Why then I'll stay at least for tea for
all the brownness is too brown and
all the whiteness too damned white
and I'm afraid
             afraid of being
any other woman's man who
might be me
             afraid
the unctuous and uneasy self I glimpse
sometimes might lose my faint and yapping cry for
being anything was never quite what I intended
And you you
             bitch no irritating
questions re love and permanence only
                an unrolling lifetime here
between your rocking thighs and
                the semblance of motion

Portrait

He was several men when I first knew him,
tho I kept hoping for one man only,
a man made of glass or stone,
heart and gizzard stamped "aging bard,"
brain logical as an x-rayed onion—
I kept trying to taunt
him into betraying himself into
being himself, prying indelicately
at the mortar that held him together
with needles, slant looks, and big bull words:
rather skeptical that Nietzsche and Lawrence
and a boy's braggadocio could make one second hand poet
or be a really effective scarecrow.
Of course he knew what I was doing,
not being stupid: made himself opaque,
or purposely pellucid to puzzle me
(at least I suppose so now),
reproving bad manners from a lily pad
healthy green in a sick frogpond.
And I grew slowly fond of him,
admired the treble profundities of lines
that no sooner said became clichés.
I believe now, however, that public utterance
and verse a minor poet can take to heart
have produced this one stone creature:
the glass man with swinging metronome appendix,
genitalia wired for sound and
howling catgut intestines with
prose secretions in bile and clacking bones—
And I admire this single man for his lavish certainties,
the onion secure in its vegetable destiny,
the long foreshortened shadow of a poet all in one place.
But then again I'm a little disappointed.

To an Ex-Wife

. . . in bed in a house in some city a woman
one I haven't seen in 10 years mutters
the long list of my shortcomings
       in her sleep and the sweaty
old quarrels—
         She leaves me a little
while before
the grey cumulus
            lifts
for coffee and red light
floods the apartment—
She curses my name and hers
at high noon
on the foot-hurting merciless streets for
the length of time it takes her
not to love the husband who shambled
       in and up to the
second hand counter after
       me:
my dear my lovely bargain—

The Machines

He sweated vomit over those
　　　　　　damn things
blood and oil on his hands
gave him a stupid dignity
like a bear smeared with garbage
The days fled into smoky weeks
and he learned to operate
one machine after another
learned them all
　　　　　　　how to gauge
the "spock" of a needle plunging
hard thru cloth beside his hand
adjusting the varied rhythms of flesh
with the balanced shifting stance of
a boxer anticipating
　　　　　　his steel opponent and
walking backward all day long
pursued
　　　　6 feet lengthways
and 4 feet 6 inches sideways

by a spastic hunchback detective
on rails urging him to confess
with metal jaws going "graff-graff"
every 2 seconds
       he managed to retain all 10
clever fingers and perhaps a soul
At the end all the submissive
hymning roar of machines praised him
for what he was
       took him for master and lord
mechanic of their metal destiny until
one afternoon he shoved a pipe-wrench
into closing jaws and heard them groan
out steel blood and shriek once
for their anthropomorphic god
              Fired
he went into the street laughing
picked up a woman near Main & Hastings
paid her $5 and went to
bed and sobbed himself
to sleep . . .

Mountain Lions
in Stanley Park

(Vancouver, B.C.)

Canadian as the Winnipeg Gold-Eye or
the Calgary Eye-Opener and
regional in this province as Strontium 90 and
international as a boundary they
lived here before night's fuses were blown—

Remember the child?
          He thought darkness had a nucleus
               something plotting
outside his range of vision something
          that moved and shambled
          laughed without logic
          and drooled—
It's rather a comfort now
to see the caged cougar's
fierce eyes focused
              serious
                 (non-idiotic) and
to be involved in the cougar's simple problems
(the snap of a bone in the head exchanging
                 light for darkness)
and walking to the edge of this floodlit concrete
not stopping at all
on the edge of the great trees—

Sun-coloured cougar
                you have forgotten the past
in this managed place where the sky
is snugged down with green tent pegs
and buildings litter the landscape
like rubble and a river of animals
hoarsely pouring down the morning
into foglit factories
                Remember quickly
the nature of boundaries—

And child of darkness
                remember the future
those strange beasts under the horizon
will want to ask questions
concerning your birthplace
                require of you
reasons for departure
deny you entry to the walking forest
Say to them
                the name is unpronounceable
                but there will be other beasts
                where I am going
We will meet there—

In the Wilderness

On the road to Agassiz in winter
of 1962
grandfathers
        young wives
                old children
marching in the savage demolitions of hunger
for their own people
to the mountain prison at Agassiz
where incendiarist husbands and
incandescent nephews and
sons of that pale yellow soap-like stuff
           which is dynamite
are locked away near a town named
for the gentle naturalist
           Louis Agassiz
In a way unrealized
these are the Children of Israel
with a Pillar of Fire by day
and a Pillar of Fire by night
standing over them in the mountains
In this wilderness
of 1962
we are all around them
(Big Fanny with sore feet slapping
onto the gravel road
Pete Elasoff with rock bruises
the old men with prophets'
beards and a Pillar of Fire
by day standing over them
on the Hope-Princeton highway
and stirrings of gravel sliding
down in the deep blue misted morning
are the trickling afterbirth of mountains)—

Note for historians:
we have set up by-laws for snares and
                deadfall regulations to trap them
the roads are shadowy with swaying nooses
                of municipal officials
the highways are luminous with Mounties and
road blocks and vote-catching grins of
                ambitious attorney generals
riding all night against these shivering foot soldiers
                slogging at dawn thru the frosty ranges—

Sitting at Agassiz with Big Fanny
in 1963
talking with Big Fanny at Agassiz
while the Mounties' "D" squad
drives by in Chevys and Pontiacs
continually hovering
talking of young Podmoroff who died
in Agassiz mountain prison and
was buried home in the Kootenays
talking of 100 men fasting and dying
in Agassiz mountain prison
the sons of mothers and daughters of husbands
and Big Fanny:
"I was 15 days on water and lemon and
now apple and prune juice"
(40 days and 40 nights in the wilderness
while the "D" squad looked and hovered
and the Pillar of Fire by day
stood over the Sons of Freedom at Agassiz)
Talking with Big Fanny
about the mystic Lebedoff
comic-opera-satan-Lebedoff
Judas-enemy of Peter Verigin's people
who plots against them in the far mountains
schemes at Wynndel
                for the people's destruction
accepting another 30 pieces of silver smiling and
the Mounties' "D" squad cruising and hovering—

(Talking to Big Fanny
making notes for an article
I think of coeval saints and ascetics and
the ordinary people with such
bright illusions of extraordinary freedom those
troublemakers of God:
could you find one in a nightclub for instance walking
across the floor and changing
                              —changing?
And how can they ever be sure they are
                    what they seem to become?
Stand up straight where the lights are glaring
bright with microphones and flashbulbs and everyone
screaming and listening and people saving
your bathwater to sell for two bucks a bottle and
raffling off your dirty underwear
at the next scheduled crucifixion and
the eyes of gentle people turning animal
—I wonder how it feels to have your plodding
pedestrian mind sprout wings and fly
handsome as an actor playing Icarus
toward the cold sun truth)—

Talking with Big Fanny
at Agassiz in 1963 sitting
on an old blue mattress cover
and she with her shoes off talking
and talking of Judas-Lebedoff
plotting against them at Wynndel
talking of exile on Piers Island
in the Gulf of Georgia in 1932
and Fanny in Kingston Pen
for 3 years in 1947-50
(did they allow her to go barefoot?)
sitting on an old blue mattress cover
with Florence Storgoff in 1963
and a Pillar of Fire by day
shining over the mountains at Agassiz
while shanties of old Kotex boxes

covered with waterproof plastic
are built near the dusty road
and the children flash by in
the running games of children laughing
and the old men with prophets' beards
stand in the road with pamphlets—
And I write in a steno's notebook
as the tourists watch and wonder
and I drink some applejuice thinking
watching the busty young females
that my thoughts are not ascetic and
Florence Storgoff all 250
pounds of her talks of persecution
and religious freedom on a side road
near Agassiz in 1963—
And the old men sing in a strange tongue
in sorrow's language over the darkening
landscape of fir trees and mountains and tremulous
whispering voices of the night animals
boom in the swamp and night birds cry over
snick of rifle bolts—
And down the road the prisoners are dying
the young hunger strikers are dying little by little—
But I am not one of them
I am not one of these people
nor do I wish to be—

    But remember their names
Verigin Elasoff Podmoroff and Big Fanny
          (with sore feet hurting)
the jubilant bombers and blazing incendiarists
the nay-sayers and Spirit Wrestlers of the Kootenay
with the Mounties' "D" squad cruising and hovering
and overhead where the mist surrounds them
a Pillar of Fire or a flash of lightning
a Pillar of Fire or only the prison floodlights—

Verigin Elasoff Podmoroff and Big Fanny
and we stand around in the wilderness watching
and we are the wilderness
                 Remember their names—

Mice in the House

One of them scampers down the curtain
and up to my motionless feet—
I have the feeling watching that
representatives of two powerful races
are meeting here calmly as equals—
But the mouse will not be damn fool enough
                to go away and write a poem—

Lu Yu (A.D. 1125-1209)

On the day of Lu Yu's last sickness
a thin coffin was ready,
and two quilts to cover him,
and the gravediggers paid
                      their work done.
Then he started to write another poem
a short time before death,
about drinking wine again in the village—
He was working on the poem when they buried him,
so that half a line protruded from the earth
                      in wind and weather's hearing—
With sunlight touching the first young syllables,
the last ones flowering from a dark coffin:
                 "marketplace the in/drink more One"
The first three words above ground
the last ones wine in the Red Dust.
Near the village of Shanyang
                      in Chekiang Province . . .

Snow at Roblin Lake

The exactitude of snow is such
that even the Eskimo
achieved mere mention of the stuff
with his 20 names for snow:

the woodpile slowly disappears
all colours blur to white
the shoremiles fade to infinite
distance in the white night—

In fifteen minutes more the house
itself is buried deep
in half an hour the world is lost
on a lazy nebular dead end street—

My little lake is not a lake
but endless ocean where I'll fish
some cosmic Tonga Trench and take
Leviathan on a bent pin—

In Sickness-

Fever and then chills
　　　body shaken and sweating thru the night
then yellow sunlight on the floor
　　　　　　　　　　　　so strange
I haven't had time to notice how light transforms
old paint that way
　　　　　　　then tossing and turning
I get interested in the way my hand looks
scar on finger
slashed from glass
　　　　　　　when I was a child
and fever allows me to remember—
And the far twitter of a sparrow
fifty feet away in a cedar
tree and a dog howling to be
let in at some farmhouse
　　　　　　　Fever and chills
　　　　　　　oranges and lemons
　　　　　　　say the bells of St. Clemon's &
　　　　　　　FeVeR aNd cHiLLs
and myself muttering thru the night
half asleep and tossing in darkness
—the darkness inside myself
full of coiling tubes & pumps & valves

my brain imprisoned atop this mindless factory
observing the faulty side effects of automation—
                    I am tucked away
                    in the blanket's corner
                    I am secreted
                    like a white candle
                    in the red darkness
                    I see the myth of God
                    is a kitchen chair
                    full of wormholes
                    and fall down and worship—
I moan peevishly for water and some hag brings it
and overwhelmed with my own intrepidity I lean
forward and drink and slobber and wonder
is that what affection
                    is a glass of water?
And stagger to the bathroom scales and
migawd I lost 8 pounds—

Morning and the birds sing and wind blows a little,
morning and it's summer—hour after hour
the sun shines hot and there's a patch of blue
leaning in the window: Oh bring me a big kettle
of elephant soup honey also a dozen great auk's
                            yellow eggs eh?
Don't say one word: just stand there with a broom
for 5 minutes while the house gets dirtier and dirtier,
just stand there all morning long and let me look at you.

Ballad of
the Despairing Wife

(After Creeley)

The time of her time was a dozen times
on a single night and she
could be heard to say she would run away
and live in a nunnery—

So we made a pact for twice a week
that's sealed with menstrual blood,
and a solemn oath that the very most
should be twice on Wednesdays once—

But the week was long ere Wednesday came
and maenad visions rose
of lesbian girls and hipster girls
and chicks in horn-rimmed glasses
and maids unclothed who turned to crones
and dolls in dream pyjamas—

On Tuesday midnight Wednesday came
and "Prithee, wife!" I said—
And knocked on the wall where the door is small,
"Do you understand?" and she did—

For love is a broken oath by day,
but sealed at night again;
no armistice yet has the least effect
on the wars of wife and man—

She finally said, "You'll wear it out,
or me or both and the bed
might well collapse and then perhaps—"
"It's tungsten steel!" I said—

And took my rhythm outside the room,
iamb and then trochee,
and dithyrambs that would not scan
were decimals of infinity—

Ere Wednesday came again the stars
had flickered their fuses down
to guttering candle stubs of flame:
they mourned an end for the human race
but signaled life from beyond the stars
back to a man at Roblin Lake:
the cosmic rays cried down at me
to people the earth and write poetry:
and the old fertility gods uprose
and called me by my name—

"Go get yourself a mistress or two
                    or a dozen or more!
                                    (she said)
I sware by the Penates and the Lares
and earth is a ball that's round
(but can't do half what you ask of yours),
I'll be a virgin a month or more
and—I'll see you in hell!"
                    (she said)—

Whereat I sware a husbandly oath
delivered with sound effects,
"The feathers shall drop from the mallard flocks
till I ask you again!" I said—

But the week was long ere Wednesday came
and there I was at the wall,
and she took me in tho love be a sin
and invented new names for God—

Oh gal my gal with the beautiful mind
I love much more than your behind,
than which however Callipygous says
is none so good till a man be dead—

And now in my mind I see the wall,
and the door beyond that beckons to me:
and it may be large or it may be small,
but it don't give a damn for poetry—

What It Was—

It was not exactly the inequalities
of schoolboy against bullying teacher
or later the fear fitting into a
strange conformity at a boarding school
or how cruelly alien boys were
—for at the time I searched out chinks
of reality in the high walls around
me and found perilous escape in books with
night flights west and sky causeways—
Later still I tore the loose membrane from
a third ear sharpening steadily now
I could never account for
and listening—

It was never either exactly when things
fell into place with a plop audible
in ordinary ears—so that at least I knew
what others thought about the general purpose
                of condoms and women
                ham and eggs
                religion and
the institution of marriage etcetera
and all the adjustments began
of deciding whether I really agreed with them

plus the dark intangibles like death and why why—
Even when bewilderment lifted a little there
was always the problem of how others acted
as against the way they said was the right way
as against the way I felt and thought was good
and making decisions by not making them
and the failure personally often
and the shame sometimes the shame
and again the listening—

Of course other problems exist here now
the necessity for patterns and pattern-makers
deciding which are certainties and which variables
(and very few of the former and mostly latter)
and always the occasional mistake
    and sometimes the brain and heart's failure
to know say
    this is the moment you'll always remember
    this is the wind-blown instant of time
    that swings you into the future
    oh heavy as the heavy cellar stones of the world
    but hammering on the gates of the sun
or merely a little older and bewildered about things
you didn't understand that perhaps meant nothing
    and fumbling to stay alive
    and always the listening—

Complaint Lodged with L.C.B.O.
by a Citizen in Upper Rumbelow

I am driving thru town with a case
of beer in the back seat
with two empties in it
which is illegal see and
I notice this cop in the rear
vision mirror following me on
a motor cycle and for a minute
I feel peculiar—
At the stop street I carefully
STOP
      and the cop stops not
to be caught that easy
and I see him watching me
sit so I sit up straight as
'The Motorist' by Praxiteles
excavated by Henry Ford 4
from under a million traffic tickets
of dead Greeks speeding in Argos agora
or was it 'Hermes' or 'Pallas Athene'
and not 'The Motorist' at all
                Anyway
there's that cop on my tail
and I signal a left turn

and he signals a left turn
I signal a right turn
and he signals a right turn
and I think what the hell
is this a game or something and
maybe didn't I brush my teeth
this morning and grin at him anyway
in the rear view mirror and figure
out a hand signal for a ground
loop and inverted immelmann plus an
unorthodox Christiana I learned
once on Parnassus which lofts
me among the treetops there encountering
God (hi pops) 50 feet above the
business section we stop to talk and
I ask him about that damned cop
of his and (ha ha) how I fooled him—

But he's parked waiting for me
at the Presbyterian steeple
that got struck by lightning like
a blue cop-angel who's a
dead ringer for the prophet Isaiah
and I says "You didn't make the turn signal"
and he says "It ain't in the book"
and I guess that's so it ain't so
I get fined fifteen bucks
and let off with a warning
but just the same—

"Malachi
Stilt-Jack Am I"

Of Santa Claus let it now be
said his
       face was a dull grey
his reindeer cannot vault even the
       smallest curbstones and
the football players
ride in colourless convertibles their
upholstery worn down
to foam rubber quivering tho it
       is still
       quite beautiful—

The pretty girls are all naturally
               virgins
their eyes are trustful
and thighs dusty
       with disuse
       but pure oh
the enthusiasm of the crowd is
       unbounded especially
high among office windows where
the upside down stenographers
       excitedly
           chew gum—

The wonderdrug discoverer is
                modestly pleased
                as would be I
                or would be you
the lion tamer bravely accepts
                adulation and
heroes of the recent glorious
war watch
the women and manage to subdue
                natural inclinations—

Later
riding thru slum clouds a dull moon
slows to a walk and stumbles down
among the confetti and gay debris
where the heroes rode for you and me
and grinning gold and grinning grey they
gallop convertibles far away to
do the things we'd like to do and
being transcendently human too
with magnificent foibles magnified
to a sort of good and a kind of pride
like character traits to mark them off
to a point we know what the difference was—

Next day
                somebody did a good deed
                all of us could recognize
                a real good deed
                and the sky was blue
                beautiful blue
I swear it was—

A Power

            to say things and
they come out of the blank
grey desert mind onto paper
trudging the heat haze then they
get away from you tho—
           and back to bed lying
beside a naked woman
(both bitch and goddess)
in the early drowsy midnight at
the dividing instant between
sleep and wakefulness between
what we know
           and don't know
           the arrow now
marking off the photographed past
and a cartoon future oh
distantly in dim cloudlands
I suppose they come from these
sideways adventurers slowly
turning into my dimension to
chuckle in darkness shoving
me out of the strange woman's bed
to shiver under a lamp at midnight
taking their weird shorthand down—
Extravagant creatures swearing
good true oaths like idiots
mouthing obscenities whipping
unbitten umbilical cords for
lassos round your throat—
            your throat?

Oh tragedian at mid day
with black circles and packed
suitcases under your eyes
(that's me?)
           all the inarticulate
afternoon waiting for evening then
your wife talking and talking of
how the long day went by and you
(that's me?) the bored husband nodding
and lapsing into a comma's
pause for supper and
television's awful semicolon until all
the lovely excommunicants come trooping
back to tell me the way it was hey
my little liars
           whispering stories about
"a country 29 days from now and we
were a long time coming here just then so
you'd better hurry along with us back there
while you can and want to
come and go with us
drunk man
drunk man"
           But why yes why?
A pride

I suppose

Optimist

In a black mood
    there seems little reason to live
after a quarrel at least
    a rejection of some kind
or when ennui fogs the lens
    you look at the world with
    and even sex dies down
    into proof of the virility
       of a habit
But it passes
    (one hemlock for the road)
         it passes
Shall we dance?

The Viper's Muse

It is portentous and a thing of state
A writes to B
            A praiseth B's poem saying
"Canada hath need of thee in this hour she
is a fen"
          etcetera etcetera
                    straightway
a second letter flieth fast to A i.e.
"Thou'rt the sweetest singer of our old
            unmusical colonial breed"
(which proveth that the pen
at least hath better manners than the sword say)
O A embarrasseth B
                with untruth
B does not dare reply unkind
            which is to say
he
    I mean that is B
               he lieth in his teeth
But whoso turns as I this night to praise
another poet partly
              partly prays
exaggeration isn't such a bloody crime
as outright lying is and was while
              Ananias'
planet riseth silent gibbous yonder
             over Parnassus

Old Alex

"85 years old, that miserable alcoholic
old bastard is never gonna die" the man said
where he got bed and board. But he did.
I'll say this about Alex' immortality tho:
if they dig him up in a thousand years
and push a spigot into his belly why
his fierce cackle'll drive a nail in silence,
his laugh split cordwood and trees kow-tow
like green butlers, the staggering world
get drunk and all the ghouls go scared—

So you say: was I fond of him?
No—not exactly anyhow. Once
he told his sons and daughters to stay away,
and then vomited on their memory. It'd be
like liking toadstools or a gun pointing at you—
He sat home three weeks drinking whiskey,
singing harsh songs and quoting verse and chapter
from the Bible: his mean and privileged piety
dying slowly: they rolled him onto a stretcher
like an old pig and prettied him with cosmetics,
sucked his blood out with a machine and
dumped him into the ground like garbage—

I don't mourn. Nobody does. Like mourning an ulcer.
Why commemorate disease in a poem then?
I don't know. But his hate was lovely,
given freely and without stint. His smallness
had the quality of making everyone else feel noble,
and thus fools. I search desperately
for good qualities and end up crawling
inside that decaying head and wattled throat
to scream obscenities like papal blessings,
knowing now and again I'm at least God—
Well, who remembers a small purple and yellow bruise long?
But when he was here he was a sunset!

Winter at Roblin Lake

Seeing the sky darken & the fields
turn brown & the lake lead-grey
as some enormous scrap of sheet metal
& wind grabs the world around the equator
I am most thankful then for knowing about
          the little gold hairs on your belly—

Hockey Players

What they worry about most is injuries
               broken arms and legs and
fractured skulls opening so doctors
can see such bloody beautiful things
almost not quite happening in the bone rooms
               as they happen outside—

And the referee?
               He's right there on the ice
not out of sight among the roaring blue gods
of a game played for passionate businessmen
and a nation of television agnostics
who never agree with the referee and applaud
when he falls flat on his face—

               On a breakaway
the centre man carrying the puck
his wings trailing a little
               on both sides why
I've seen the aching glory of a resurrection
               in their eyes
               if they score
but crucifixion's agony to lose
—the game?

               We sit up there in the blues
bored and sleepy and suddenly three men
break down the ice in roaring feverish speed and
we stand up in our seats with such a rapid pouring
of delight exploding out of self to join them why
theirs and our orgasm is the rocket stipend

for skating thru the smoky end boards out
of sight and climbing up the appalachian highlands
and racing breast to breast across laurentian barrens
over hudson's diamond bay and down the treeless
                                        tundra where
auroras are tubercular and awesome and
stopping isn't feasible or possible or lawful
but we have to and we have to
                                    laugh because we must and
stop to look at self and one another but
                    our opponent's never geography
                                or distance why
            it's men
            —just men?

And how do the players feel about it
this combination of ballet and murder?
For years a Canadian specific
to salve the anguish of inferiority
by being good at something the Americans aren't—
And what's the essence of a game like this
which takes a ten year fragment of a man's life
replaced with love that lodges in his brain
                    and takes the place of reason?
Besides the fear of injuries
is it the difficulty of ever really overtaking
a hard black rubber disc?
Is it the impatient coach who insists on winning?
Sportswriters friendly but sometimes treacherous?
—And the worrying wives wanting you to quit and
your aching body stretched on the rubbing table
thinking of money in owner's pocket that might be in yours
the butt-slapping camaraderie and the self indulgence
of allowing yourself to be a hero and knowing
everything ends in a pot-belly—

Out on the ice can all these things be forgotten
in swift and skilled delight of speed?
—roaring out the endboards out the city
streets and high up where laconic winds
whisper litanies for a fevered hockey player—
Or racing breast to breast and never stopping
over rooftops of the world and all together
sing the song of winning all together
sing the song of money all together . . .

          (and out in the suburbs
there's the six year old kid
whose reflexes were all wrong
who always fell down and hurt himself and cried
and never learned to skate
              with his friends)—

Peonies Beside the Lake

We fed them potato peelings and rotten meat
we fed them fermented garbage for 5 years
while the stems sickened
                  and leaves turned yellow
we fed them garden fertilizer and horseshit
begged from the only farmer with horses for miles
We gave what women have sometimes given
who have no sons and mourn their lost children
                  in the menses of growing things
which bear no fruit and cannot be eaten
                  except by tongues of the eyes
—or the gentleness of senility in very old women
who really do not know why something aches
inside them when a flower is born
as we are ignorant of our own motives
                  after such a long time waiting
to see how the new peonies shine
                  reddening the dull lake water

Home-Made Beer

I was justly annoyed 10 years ago
in Vancouver: making beer in a crock
under the kitchen table when this
next door youngster playing with my own
kid managed to sit down in it and
emerged with one end malted—
With excessive moderation I yodelled
at him
        "Keep your ass out of my beer!"
       And the little monster fled—
Whereupon my wife appeared from the bathroom
where she had been brooding for days
over the injustice of being a woman and
attacked me with a broom—
With commendable savoir faire I broke
the broom across my knee (it hurt too) and
then she grabbed the breadknife and made
for me with fairly obvious intentions—

I tore open my shirt and told her calmly
with bared breast and a minimum of boredom
        "Go ahead! Strike! Go ahead!"
Icicles dropped from her fiery eyes as she
snarled
            "I wouldn't want to go to jail
              for killing a thing like you"
I could see at once that she loved me
tho it was cleverly concealed—
For the next few weeks I had to distribute
the meals she prepared among neighbouring
dogs because of the rat poison and
addressed her as Missus Borgia—
That was a long time ago and while
at the time I deplored her lack of
self control I find myself sentimental about
it now for it can never happen again—

Sept. 22, 1964.   P.S. I was wrong—

Dylan

Before his death all the women
outside the hospital outside
the oxygen tent wrangling and
Caitlin going mad a little
when he stopped breathing and
prosy Brinnin writing his
book about apocalyptic Dylan
(Dylan the sneak-thief who
loved every woman who wasn't
his wife and got disgustingly
drunk and died one day)
telling the whole truth
the whole truth for nothing
for nothing but money and death
and death becoming a best seller—

But his children will keep in
their loins a vision of
the wild futile man from
Swansea tho they have
forgotten the slobbering
drunk who died and others
will die in the agony of
some grey hospital and
live in live green tales a
moment and they too will be
dead in a moment and they too
will be once and soon
alive in whiskey summer they
too alive
            in an oxygen tent for knowing
their only world is dying outside and
            they too will be
born in an oxygen tent tho
once and soon the world is dying—

One Rural Winter

Trapped
     cut off
          marooned
like a city thief sentenced to a country jail
the rural mail my only communication with outside
surrounded by nothing
          but beautiful trees
          & I hate beautiful trees
I'm lost beyond even the remote boundaries
of Ameliasburg
      & I ask you
what could be more remote than a burg
named after someone
      named Amelia?
Why just close your eyes hard out here
and you don't see little dots of light
      you see fresh cowpads

But it's winter now
      beyond the economic wall
(I have two nickels a dime and quarter
and not a damn cent
in my pockets but a wife
who comes out when I'm asleep
and won't meet the burning stare
of my closed dreaming womanless eyes
      she's a damn coward that's all)

      In the backyard
pieces of wood and stones embedded in ice
(notice the Freudian terminology please)
I'm trapped forever in the 3rd Post-Atomic Glacial Period
(making witty remarks like "Cold out, ain't it, Zeke?")
It's got so I'm even afraid to go outside

I might catch my foot in a lateral moraine or something
and be trapped forever in Ameliasburg Township
a pillar of saltlick slowly melting away
                    melting away
from a cow's tongue and gazing wistfully from
her digestive tract bitten by stomach bugs
like rinderpest and Spanish fly
but gazing wistfully I say
                    nor' nor' east to Montreal
where my friends are laughing and making love
                    to women

The earth is frozen
the beautiful trees are frozen
even the mailbox is frozen
& I'm getting a little chilly myself
living in a house I built with Unemployment Insurance
                    and pounded thumbnails
But I got into this mess myself
and I ain't blamin the class struggle
Besides there's a girl where I'm going now
on a ten mile trek to the shithouse
She's waiting for me and improving her mind
reading the reader's digest toiletpaper
till I get there half an hour from now
where my most delicate imagining placed her
right over the hole
                    Move darling
room for the factotum
and less noise while we're reading please
Then plunging back to the house
thru skull-deep snow alone
                              the WIND
steals all my internal heat
my heavy body is doped with wind and cold
              and the house door
              drags me into the hall
              and the door knob
is a handle I hold onto the sky with

Old Settler's Song[#]

I've travelled all over the country,
prospectin and diggin for gold,
I've tunneled, hydraulicked and cradled,
and I have been frequently sold!
Ah yes,—been frequently sold!
I've tunneled, hydraulicked and cradled
for reasons I'd rather weren't told—
                         (Ah-ha?)
But I have been frequently sold!
Singin tooralai—ooralai—ooralai O,
there's a mountain of gold in the far Cariboo!

There's a pass that leads thru the mountains,
there's a valley I saw in my dreams:
if you go there with guts and a shovel
you'll come back fartin nuggets they say—
But a poor man I went thru the mountains,
and a rich man I never will be,
lyin buried deep under the mountains,
a poor man forever I'll stay.
Singin tooralai—ooralai—ooralai O,
there's plenty of gold in the far Cariboo
for the ones that come later
           the ones that always come later
                   much later than we
                         (Ho-ho!)—
Singin tooralai—ooralai—ooralai O,
there's a mountain of gold in the far Cariboo!

[#]Old song, of which I have left very little
but the title and chorus.

Roblin's Mills

The mill was torn down last year
and stone's internal grey light
gives way to new green
a shading of surface colour
like the greenest apple of several—
The spate of Marthas and Tabithas
   incessant Hirams and Josephs
is stemmed in the valley graveyard
where the censored quarrels of loving
and the hatred and by golly gusto
of a good crop of buckwheat and turnips
end naturally as an agreement between friends
(in the sandy soil that would grow nothing
but weeds or feed a few gaunt cattle)
and the spring rain takes their bodies
a little deeper down each year
   maybe the earliest settlers
some stern Martha or speechless Joseph
perhaps meet and mingle
   1000 feet down—
And the story about the grist mill
rented in 1914 to a man named Taylor
by the last of the Roblin family
who demanded a share of the profits:

       the lighting Alters
and you can see
      how a bald man stood
sturdily indignant
      and spat on the ground
and stamped away so hard the flour
dust floated out from his clothes
like a white nimbus round his body
beneath the red scorn—
              Those old ones
you can hear them on a rural party line
sometimes
      when the copper wires
sing before the number is dialed and
then your own words stall some distance
from the house you said them in
      lost in the 4th concession
      or dimension of whatever
      a lump in your throat
      an adam's apple
      half a mile down the road
      permits their voices
      to float by
      on the party line sometimes
      and you hang up then
      so long now—

Fidel Castro
in Revolutionary Square

He begins to speak
(a million people listening):
and I wonder what it's like
to be that careless young student
in Havana drinking beer
with his friends until
something pops in his mind
and he stands up:
                              "I've decided
to take over the country.
                              I'll need help."
The fragile intention flees
from face to face like fever
becomes a condition of existence
a thought to think when first
putting on your pants in the morning
and the faces gather around him
and the high talk begins—
And a stranger sits down again
not the same young student
not the same man
and three hours later
the speech ends—

Everyone joins hands and sings together
a million voices and bodies
sway back and forth in the sunlight
and make some remark about being human
addressed to no one exactly
spoken to no imperialist
snarled at no invader
as natural as eating supper
that is able to touch the future
and fill an emptiness
and fills an emptiness in the future—
Or else that's another illusion
something nice to believe in
the continuity of people
a we/they and me/you concept
as saccharine as religion
to comfort a world of children
with proletarian lullabies—
A million people move to the exits
under a sky of passionate emptiness
returning to the fact of duration
and chicken hearts in nutritive solution
and glands living the good life
                    in a test tube
the great ambiguity the last cliché—
And back at the shining Cadillac
we came in (Batista's old car)
under the side where I hadn't
noticed before the body
of a small dead animal—

                    Cuba May 1st, 1964

The Country
North of Belleville

Bush land scrub land—
        Cashel Township and Wollaston
Elvezir McClure and Dungannon
green lands of Weslemkoon Lake
where a man might have some
        opinion of what beauty
is and none deny him
                for miles—

Yet this is the country of defeat
where Sisyphus rolls a big stone
year after year up the ancient hills
picnicking glaciers have left strewn
with centuries' rubble
                days in the sun
when realization seeps slow in the mind
without grandeur or self deception in
                noble struggle
of being a fool—

A country of quiescence and still distance
a lean land
          not fat
with inches of black soil on
          earth's round belly—
And where the farms are it's
          as if a man stuck
both thumbs in the stony earth and pulled

                    it apart to make room
enough between the trees
for a wife
          and maybe some cows and
          room for some
of the more easily kept illusions—
And where the farms have gone back
to forest
          are only soft outlines and
          shadowy differences—
Old fences drift vaguely among the trees
          a pile of moss-covered stones
gathered for some ghost purpose
has lost meaning under the meaningless sky
          —they are like cities under water and
the undulating green waves of time are
          laid on them—

This is the country of our defeat and
       yet
during the fall plowing a man
might stop and stand in a brown valley of the furrows
       and shade his eyes to watch for the same
       red patch mixed with gold
       that appears on the same
       spot in the hills
       year after year
       and grow old
plowing and plowing a ten acre field until
the convolutions run parallel with his own brain—

And this is a country where the young
          leave quickly
unwilling to know what their fathers know
or think the words their mothers do not say—

Herschel Monteagle and Faraday
lakeland rockland and hill country
a little adjacent to where the world is
a little north of where the cities are and
sometime
we may go back there
              to the country of our defeat
Wollaston Elvezir Dungannon
and Weslemkoon lake land
where the high townships of Cashel
           McClure and Marmora once wer
But it's been a long time since
and we must enquire the way
        of strangers—

"A Very Light Sort of Blue
Faded from Washing"

I was thinking of him this morning
as if we'd been lovers
     (as some thought we were, no doubt:
homosexuals sniggering from lamppost
to lamppost
         like dogs looking for shadows
         the same shape as their bodies)
It occurs to me
I wouldn't be thinking the way I am
if we hadn't been in some sense and
         love of male for male becomes
not a broken pane of glass in the soul
or only permissable after death
          as Alec is
(where love also is barred entrance
a whisper stops at death's frontier
—8 diatonic degrees above or below
the octave cannot penetrate those borders
not ballistæ or hydrogen locksmiths
can sesame open those gates nor one
soft decibel of human music
         slip thru)
—becomes this strange remembering
I have for people
        well call it love

But Alec now
                in bed with damp earth
and it grieves me a little that no woman
is there to make the worms more interesting
                and no friend
but one like myself who shambles into memory
as if it were the streets of a strange town
at night turning a corner lost and looking
for someone I know and finding
                —finding no one

Oh I remember talking and laughing
and the terribly bad poems he wrote
                and Alec saying:
"I don't think they're very good
                (and they weren't)
        but I've got to try,
        don't you think so?"
I would have answered then while
we were standing just outside the
door of his rooming house with
myself getting ready to leave
                and he said:
"They're not very good.
                I can't give them
anything that's inside me—"
He jerked his fingers at the blue pullover
he was wearing and started to close the door:
"Perhaps I can get this blue down on paper.
I'm gonna try anyway,
                and maybe after I'm dead—"
The word startled me and I said:
                "After you're dead, Alec?"
But the door swung closed/
                "Goodnight—"

Death of John F. Kennedy

On first hearing of his death
no one believed it
          not for a moment
                for 3 years
television and newspapers
had made him a god of our time
and gods are indestructible
          But he was only a man
and the man has quietly removed himself
leaving behind the uninhabited legend
of himself which is a little like
an empty suit of armour made
by a Bronx tailor for maybe
Richard Coeur de Lion—

He (Kennedy) was one of the famous
for whom poems get written like
Dylan Thomas—Roosevelt—Nicolai Lenin—
(only during their dying lifetime of course)
And of those three only Thomas had the
endearing fictional qualities of being
real most of the time 24 hours later than
the 2nd hand reported outrageous events
of his life and
          I mourn for Caitlin who
in jigtime undeniably becomes
fiction and has a ghostlike sound

And come to think of it
                    I mourn Lee Oswald
                    as well as Kennedy who
was a normal sort of social do-gooder god whereas
Oswald is prototype of the deranged assassin
                    He murdered Caesar and Lincoln
                    Archduke Ferdinand and all those titles
                    even attempted Hitler
and just the other day downtown
in a poolroom made a pass at me—
                    Yes
                    I mourn Lee Oswald
because he was a kind of Typhoid Mary
who had the disease in its pure form
one disease we all have
                    ANIMAL HATE
that seems so handcuffed to human vitality
so linked and hogtied to the best things
If Oswald had lived
perhaps we could have isolated it
in a test tube
                    labelled "Oswald Extract"
or "Very Dangerous" and "Much Too Human"
part of the obscure pride and shame
of being homo sapiens that might be used
to cross the galaxies—

                    (Is that why I mourn Lee Oswald?
because he was much too human?
and as a result was never alive?
Typhoid Mary with a high-powered mailorder rifle
infecting future colonies across the nebulae
with hate
                    Hey—if only I'd killed Oswald
in the poolroom downtown when I had my chance
                    See what I mean?)

And thinking
how the mind empties of passion and speculation
how the population of earth is replaced
every hundred years the Caesars and street cleaners
and fathers and mothers and painfully awkward
adolescents with pimples without furore and
no one escapes in the outcry only
pyramids and some broken bits of pottery
survive the long howl of a funeral oration
        and out in the suburbs all the time
a mother of six
      is quietly having another baby—

      And I mourn Kennedy
      the man everybody knows
—strangers who never met
connected by a dead man's compass points
and vectors penetrating now
        like battery terminals:
for which the power supply
jams under a heavy load of messages from
hunstsmen falling asleep standing in snowstorms
in the 2nd Ice Age forever and Sumerian shepherd
kings catching cold and dead of the sniffles and
messages from rock cairns in Transylvania
and exiles in a Roman province from Hyannisport
and Sierra Maestra and Crimea and silence:
for which the power supply
is an inflection of a subordinate clause
      on television
      a remembered grin—

Bums and Brakies

(1937)

They and we come over the singing
tracks and you can't tell the difference
between us at dawn with faces
dirty from cinders and eyes
sore from watching the black foetus
locomotive ahead born monstrous
inside our skulls every morning
and the smoke stack vomiting golden
angels sometimes
        Now plodding the cinders
dozens and hundreds of men from railways
in Sioux Lookout and Blind River
and Piapot Saskatchewan and
Summerland Medicine Hat and
Tulameen and Stoney Lonesome (and
never where they want to be for
empty pockets and other

membranes round the heart cut them
off from home) who scatter among
greasy all-night restaurants
for coffee and sitting there for
a nickel's worth of not being alone
often not bothering to wash on
red stools
        The town cop comes
in with a railway bull and both
stare round them suspiciously and
the railway workers keep drinking
their coffee with little gritty
gulps washing down cinders and
soft phlegm and maybe
           blood and the bums
stiffen bent over the counter almost
sure that nothing is about to happen
& knowing they don't look much like railwaymen
(cops can always tell the difference)
& wonder if they're even very human
& have no way of knowing—

Potter

I

Scots-Irish and wearing a leather apron,
with a lame foot he got in the war;
works for the tourist trade from
9 to 5—seldom longer,
except for special orders of course.
Paints maple leaves under the glaze,
beaver and hockey players maybe;
if the price is right your very own face
on a beer mug—or John Macdonald
may be had for an honest dollar—
Has the potter a soul?
For that come back in another century.

Still, it's quite possible,
one with some harmless dust on it
for which no one's made an offer yet.
If they had he might not sell,
or hold out for a better offer,
since Faust brought the price down somewhat—
Still
        no one's made him an offer,
        not in this century . . .

II

Come back again when it isn't raining—
What's there to see now with
the kids in the car and wife complaining
about getting back to Toronto
before closing time at the stores—
But maybe he doesn't want to
go and just stands there thinking
about—well it doesn't matter
much in all these miles of watery
weather
            certainly not Toronto
or anywhere exactly
not in this century . . .

III

. . . a saucer-eyed Sumerian
patting pottery buttocks as
if there was a young girl's body
in the wet clay under
                        deep under
those laughing long-dead 5000 year old hands . . .

IV

. . . an apprentice from Kiangsi province
lying down to sleep in kiln dust
with a few snowflakes falling
thinking
   not of Chang Ch'ien sailing
   a log down the Milky Way
   or himself plunging into the fire
   to make a red bowl for
   some emperor
being only an apprentice
homesick for the wet green
of Kiangsi province
lying down to sleep in the hot dust . . .

V

    Again on the highway
to Toronto or somewhere
    in this century
or another one sometime with
    hot dogs and ice cream
for sale by the roadside and
    cars shoot by
(I think that was Pickering)
    in the rain and kids
asleep in the back seat and mother
    love eternal in the front seat
and she'll make it in time
    she's bound to make it in time
before the stores close
at closing time in Toronto
when the lights go out in Toronto
    this century or another one . . .

Country Snowplow

              Tyrannosaurus
comes lumbering around the stalled
Quaternary glaciers to deliver his ancient
                thundering manifesto
modified to suit the times—
             Tyrannosaurus
roaming the bed clothes of earth—
Warm in the cold hutch rabbits endure
their scarcities
          owls survive a dream
of pterodactyls—
       SNOW
engendering in marsupial darkness
the fierce equations of light—
             To rescue
the perishing
        married woman expecting
strength from snowshovel husband
he knowing and searching the shapes of self
to seize the disparate ghost that strength is
baby about to be born or old man dying
without help
        in diesel thunder
the transistor's and sick woman's bones
      dance
         neuter together—

Others
      with all the resources of not-needing
(the white dust being merely white dust) hold
steadfast in the pouring
                  millrace of cold
marshal around them magazines
                      collections of postage stamps
and all the old absorbing hobbies of
                  getting and keeping and counting
barricade themselves in themselves and
wait
      indignant at the lateness of the hour—
                  Thunder dies
and in the monster's milky wake
                  come separate and severally
the chattering mammals—

Observer

The sun stripes half the winter trees
with lengthways light
                leaving the other half shadowed
I notice suddenly
        the sun the trees and I
are a triangle
                of which
I can actually see very little
A sparrow abandons flight
                        for a perch
on high branches making
            the silver isosceles tip
        a shuddering omphalos
                for bird watchers

I curse myself for this madman's frenzy
that wants to make pretty patterns
cut from life
            Tomorrow I'll get roaring drunk
and tell tremendous lies to myself
                        for an hour
and wistfully yearn for the sober truth
                        of these
polygonal dichotomous rectangular hexametric
        —trees
                and myself
                        for an hour

Double Talk

tho we lie as lovers
your body shaking against my lips
                              your hair wet
novae bursting at the bedroom window
typewriter downstairs pecking polka dots in eternity
our bodies covered with sweat
                 our minds with perspiration
                 of beautiful thoughts but
                 the wine we drink nevertheless
       tastes bad

our bodies fly at each other
       glance off
       become all
of a million volte faces of light or
40 watts peeking in under the bedroom door more
       or less
       your hair wet
       as love does to one
or two as the case may be nevertheless
the typewriter downstairs cudgels away on one edge
of an incident
                 the outer edge of a vague gentleness then
protrudes on this side of love's patient savagery
                              and stops

but outside
                the stars are fucking the universe and
the visiting novae sneak off hysterically
                to the Lesser Magellanic Cluster there
                to consult a good gynecologist

and
        don't touch me for a minute
        you're shaking
        I can't help it
        but why
        leave me alone
        have a cigarette
        if it comes to that
        how do the words go
        what words
        the ones about
        the beginning
        or the end and
        the poignancy of
        a fragment imagined
        as entirety but
        you said
        I know that
        I know it too
        This poem then

To an Attempted Suicide

(At Sunnybrook Hospital)

What can I do for you
          my friend?
Will you try again soon?
Is the goddam world that desolate?
          —thrown away cigarette butts
          picked up by bums and
          people's lives nobody
          picks up—

This robbery of all you thought valuable
          committed in private
          committed by a woman
—isn't it maybe possible that such a theft allows
          unnoticed things of no value and
          visible for the first time to
Gleam
          gold
                in a chill sun?

(This curious creature
behind bars at a military zoo
watched closely by attendants
as the pendulum swings back and
forth between here and death
euphoria and black depression
alternating bouts with Jacob's angel
and the eyes of visiting spectators
swivel left and right for tennis tho
who wins arouses much disinterest and
someone says hell I'm interested—
But you can't prove it
                can you mister?)

You self pitying slob you
stupid bastard I can talk rings around (and
leave uncircled the silence of things) who
thought he was so irresistible women melted
under his loins after the words' boom was
always previously and primarily still there oh yes
                you roaring at the bourgeois
                or just ranting-silly and
                so beautifully—
I can love a man with such a splendid weakness
                for a woman
                crying jag for the world's
                hurt people and
                if I talk too fast
                blinded by arrogance
angry at all unchangeable things that happen
myself grown tired
                of the long
                humiliation of living
                nevertheless
will you please continue to stand there for a while
                with that dumb look
                of the world's enduring losers those
continual spendthrifts of their mortal selves
—stand somewhere in imagination's distance
                from your foolish dreams and
                        halfway back to here from there
                                sustain me with your presence
                                        —my friend?

Homo Canadensis

I didn't know him
        but thought somebody else did,
for everyone was friendly in that bar
           except this guy in the red checked shirt:
he was aggressive and pro-Canadian,
stubbing a Players outside the ashtray,
swaying in his chair and gulping beer
like water
        drunk and getting drunker—
"Best beer in the world," he said.
"Bout the only thing left that's really Canadian."
           And glared at us.
"Did you know 60% of Canadian industry
           is American owned?
They callem American shubshidyaries—"
Everyone laughed when he stumbled over the word,
and he slapped his hand hard on the table,
"Don't laugh!" he said.
"Okay, I been drinkin, I like to drink.
But don't laugh when you see this country
TAKEN OVER
        just sort of casually
like an afterthought, like a burp after dinner—"
        "So what?" somebody said.
"Everybody here knows we'll belong to the States
        in another 10 years . . ."
The guy swelled up like a sneering bullfrog,
"And guys like you deserve to be taken over.
But when you are you'll be 2nd class Americans,
like Negroes in the south, like Indians here—
You'll be 2nd class Americans because
you were never 1st class Canadians in the first place—"
Everybody stiffened.

                    "Okay," he said,
"I'll buy the beer and shut up."
But after a few seconds he couldn't keep quiet.
"Anybody ever hear of the San Juan Islands?
No, I guess not. Well, Canada got gypped there.
Anybody know about the Alaska Panhandle deal,   .
or remember the Herbert Norman case, by any chance?
Well, I'm tellin you, this country is being taken
like a glass of beer. It's a matter of economics.
And none of you guys really give a damn,
just slop your beer and wait to be taken
by some big bellied American in Washington.
And I'm tellin you, they're all greedy bastards—!"
"I like Americans," someone said mildly,
and it seemed just by chance his arm lifted,
meeting checked shirt's arm in the middle of the table.
That was all it needed:
"Okay, loud mouth, let's see you put me down!"
They call it "arm wrestling" some places:
and the yellow beer jiggled as clasped hands
pushed on elbow fulcrum—everyone watching.
The guy in the checked shirt was drunk
and the other guy more or less sober,
so it shouldn't have been much of a contest.
Their arms strained like two-thirds of a tripod,
and checked shirt put on the pressure,
"I'm tellin you they're bastards—!"
The other guy was big, but he collapsed quick,
knocking over a glass of beer and the salt shaker.
"Just shows you," checked shirt said,
looking around the table. He started to go.
"I gotta be gettin back. Be seein ya—"
"You been huntin?" somebody asked.
"That's right, up near Bancroft. Takin back a nice buck."
"Where ya from?"
Checked shirt grinned.
"New York," he said.

Wine-Maker's Song

After a while the grapes confer
among themselves
            begin to whisper
marvellous bubbling secrets together
which they may divulge
            in a few weeks
inlook and outsight of the coloured cosmos
and philosophic tilting pinball planets
seen scarcely often only upside down and
            (they'll fool you)
            sometimes sideways endwise
sweetly by
            the gentle gutter connoisseurs—
They may divulge excitedly
            with tenor and soprano whispers why
the bottle necking wisdom sounds so
            harsh and hoarsely in
continent men's ears and in
coherent to such and such and sober so and sos
            and cry
"We are the dead
drunk short hours ago
we truly serious and sober looked you
straight in your damned eyes while asking terribly
            'How are you?' "
            like any other stranger—

begin to whisper
inlook and outsight of the coloured cosmos
and how illusions seem to end while walking tall
                        beneath the kitchen table
and all our real and unreal selves decide themselves
                  which one is human
and stumble out in search of what they are
and stagger out among the uniforms to
issue proclamations to the world
and drunken manifestoes made of poem-dust and eon-mist
that say the way things ought to be
and how the drab grey rules and regs of kings and pricks
                      and man's morality
Stop
    short
        wait
             behind a mouthful of wet commas till
            until you say or I do anyway
no need of further questions to yourself to
one woman woman
                now
                    this part of me is part of me
my dear and certainly
most certainly
this at least
        is what I am—

I Think It Was Wednesday

2 miles of dusty road to the village
and me on it
     a fairly young man walking and counting
zigs of zagging snake fences
loyalist farmers measured long ago
chased by points and limits and dimensions—
  How many miles to Alexandria
from dusty Ameliasburg?
  How far would Euclid make it?
       —counting the zigs and zags and odds
and evens
      in   like
        and out   numeral music—
  You could grow old walking to the village
or sailing to Alexandria over the yellow wheat
to buy hamburger and dates in the bazaar
at Alexandria or Ameliasburg
jostled by Euclid and Ptolemy
come sweating into the sunlight
        from classroom and palace—
Old loverboy
Euclid wooing the last unbroken virgin
the highest numerical prime—
  Did he find her before the muezzin sounded
that spindly love-starved creature with round
       Os for thighs
searching for her divisor in the bloodless
      passionless skies?

Or come counting with me the loyalist fences
and drag Ptolemy along on the road to a dusty village
far far from anywhere they knew
                    stand without surprise
labelling the zigs and zags
—3-5-7-11-13-17
                    how high?
  Here we are
                    Euclid and Ptolemy and I
walking along the dusty road to a village
pinned down like bugs in the definite here
and now and numbers
                    prime numbers
go rocketing outbound over and under
my head and feet and Ptolemy's tinsel crown
looks a bit battered as if he'd slept in it and
Euclid's beard hasn't been combed—
  "Euc, old boy (I say)
  here's a good touch for you:
  I'm gonna make each prime number
  to the power of p,
  and of course that's me.
  Like this
          —3p-5p-7p-11p-13p-17p
                              like that.
  We're here
              (I told him and he caught on fast),
  we're here, but the prime numbers
  keep on going somewhere,
  each to the power of me,
  if you'll forgive the vanity, Euc.
  We're finite, but numbers aren't—
  Get it, boy?"

Suddenly there was snow in the zags of the snake fences
in the zigs it was still summer
and we were getting a little old
as the numbers slipped over the canning factory hill
in the zigs among rotting tomato peelings—
    In the zags by the airport an old fashioned jet plane
warmed up in the snow—
    And the numbers
                        prime numbers
reeled away in the sky
where it never
                    once was
                    Wednesday
into a silence untouched by names of things—
    The numbers
                        prime numbers
got tangled up in Aquarius
and star rivers of Eridanus
                            broke free
of the canning factory to Perseus and Ursus Major
and we were left there just
Ptolemy and Euclid and I
standing on the road—
    And pretty soon there was only myself
walking to Ameliasburg
                        an old man
pinned down in the definite
held like a bug in the finite
chased by points and limits and dimensions
walking the long road to a village
and overhead the stars beginning to—

Late Rising
at Roblin Lake

All hours the day begins one may
awake at dawn with bird cries
streaking light to sound to song
to coloured silence wake with
sun stream shuttle threading thru
curtain shadows dazzling eyes at
4 p.m. and 9 p.m. and 1 a.m. one May
awake inside a moving house earthbound
by heart tick and clockbeat only all
one August afternoon once why
stumbling yawning nude to front
window there on the dock
        in noon fog lit
with his own slow self-strangeness
stood a tall blue heron

       and the day began with him—

Cronos at the
Quinte Hotel

In the tavern
I asked the 92
year old man what it was like
to be what he was
and tentatively is
(how does it feel
to have your body become
a bag of old flesh
carried round by bones?)
asked if any sex was
left when a girl jiggled
past He got mad and made
to blast me like Zeus only
with fists
I cowered
from his lightning
realizing without thought
that nobody but bernard shaw
could hit a 92 year old
man But he changed his mind

the imperial old fists

       fell

harmless and for a moment
I knew what it was like
       to be old so old
even bernard shaw's beard is boyfuzz
         I knew what it was like
When the old man left leaving
a nickel tip for the waiter he
left strutting and as young as ah
—young as a newborn fossil and
       he walked straight

I remember a short month later
going downtown and a warm sun
on my neck shone in the middle
of a long afternoon looking
at a young girl's legs and
I chuckled as
      softly as a fossil might
if a fossil could by god
chuckle watching how I walked
from shop window to shop
window and
       I walked straight—

John

We go out to visit John—
He owns a big dance hall with a
lighted waterfall and a ship at
one end for the paying customers
to pretend with—
And he has a bathtub in his basement
full of 12 inch goldfish some
workmen found in a quarry which
he intends to blend and make part of
the décor—

He talks of the ancient Greek philosophers
(his kick is Hellenic right now)
the soaring architecture and literature
the oral-sexual routine of hetaerae
are all his own personal discoveries—
John says Canada is nothing compared to Greece
and everyone talks at once arguing the
point and nobody ever finishes a sentence—
I can understand why he thinks how he thinks
comparing his own artificial waterfall
and the ruins of Periclean Athens
comparing Sophocles' Oedipus cycle
to this then-unwritten poem of mine
about a dance hall owner talking
about Socrates drinking bitter hemlock
while I watch the saliva glitter
after he licks his lips—

My Grandfather Talking
—30 Years Ago

Not now boy not now
some other time I'll tell ya
what it was like
the way it was
without no streets
or names of places round
an nothin but moonlight boy
nothin but that

Why ain't there woods no more?
I was usta woods an
how far was anywhere was
as far as the woods went
ceptin up
          an I never went

They put a road there
an a girl on the road
in a blue dress
an given a place to go
from I went
into the woods with her
it bein the best way
to go an never get there

Walk in the woods an not get lost
wherever the woods go
a house in the way
a wall in the way
a stone in the way
that got there quick as hell
an a man shouting stop
but you don't dast stop
or everything would fall down
You low it's time boy
when you can't tell anyone
when there ain't none to tell
about whatever it was I was sayin
what I was talkin about
what I was thinkin of—?

Transient

Riding the boxcars out of Winnipeg in a
morning after rain so close to
the violent sway of fields it's
like running and running
naked with summer in your mouth and
the guy behind you grunts and says
"Got a smoke?"

Being a boy scarcely a moment and you
hear the rumbling iron roadbed singing
under the wheels at night and a door jerking open
mile after dusty mile riding into Regina with
the dust storm crowding behind you and
a guy you hardly even spoke to
nudges your shoulder chummily and says
"Got a smoke?"

Riding into the Crow's Nest mountains with
your first beard itching and a
hundred hungry guys fanning out thru
the shabby whistlestops for handouts and
not even a sandwich for two hundred miles
only the high mountains and knowing
what it's like to be not quite a child
any more and listening to the tough men
talk of women and talk of the way things are
in 1937

Riding down in the spit-grey sea level morning
thru dockyard streets and dingy dowager houses
with ocean a jump away and the sky beneath you
in puddles on Water Street and an old Indian woman
pushing her yawning scratching daughter
onto a balcony to yell at the boy-man passing

"Want some fun?—come on up" and the girl just
come from riding the shrieking bedspring bronco
all the up and down night to a hitchpost morning
full of mothers and dirt and lice and
            hardly the place for a princess
            of the Coast Salish
                        (My dove my little one
tonight there will be wine and the loins of a dozen men
to pin you down in the outlying lands of sleep
innocent as a child
            awaiting the last of all your bridegrooms)

Stand in the swaying boxcar doorway
moving east away from the sunset and
after a while the eyes digest a country and
the belly perceives a mapmaker's vision
in dust and dirt on the face and hands here
its smell drawn deep thru the nostrils down
to the lungs and spurts thru blood stream
campaigns in the lower intestine
            and chants love songs to the kidneys
After a while there is no arrival and
no departure possible any more
you are where you were always going
and the shape of home has planted itself in your loins
the identity of forests that were always nameless
the selfhood of rivers that are changing always
the nationality of riding a boxcar thru the depression
over long green plains and high mountain country
with the best and worst of a love that's not to be spoken
and a guy right behind you says then
"Got a smoke?"
You give him one and stand in the boxcar doorway
or looking out the window of a Montreal apartment
or running the machines in a Vancouver factory
—you stand there growing older

The Old Girl Friend

We made love in a parked cemetery
with youthful uneasiness
about the stationary dead
                After marriage
I sat between them at a movie
holding hands with both
chuckling polygamous and evil
at this beginning of having enough of women
Now my laughter at all my selves
includes our meeting at 40
with somnolent gossip of middle-aged certainties tho
never now the goose girl wondering what came next
and which hand was which and where but never
why in a parked car while the dead talked
softly whatever the dead discuss
Never the goose girl now or gander lout
            from
            1940
who made a jewelled baldric from a sweat shirt
and simmering flesh imperishable as grass roots
and a silver bugle from a jalopy's horn
that kept going "Yippee Yippay"
all night long
in the catacombs of moonlight
among the tombs of tumescent corpses
until a dead spinster complained
she couldn't sleep
and the old caretaker
came

Helping My Wife Get Supper

Something basically satisfying real and valid
about being a husband
brandishing a knife and cutting
up soggy tomatoes
                        not just red
but red all through
And there's something undeniably profound about
                        being red all through
like a cavalry charge in the salad
But I could get indignant at this lettuce
for allowing itself to be sliced
by somebody's husband like so much dead meat
                        not making a move
to defend itself just
lying there limply relying on being green
Not like the onion
                        which is not defenseless
                        for nobody makes friends with an onion
                        except another one
                        and then they don't trust each other
                        like two skunks
And the carrot's such a bright orange orange
it ought to be more than just a carrot
which anyway is a futile condition to be in
and it might be better not to be a carrot
if you could manage to get out of it
                        be warned beforehand
you were liable to be somebody's husband
                        but nobody ever is

Method For
Calling Up Ghosts

Walking sometimes in the streets of the town
I live in and thinking of all the people who
lived here once and fill the space I fill—
If they'd painted white trails on the sidewalk
everywhere they went, it would be possible
to see them now.
                        Imagine them as line drawings,
and at once they become visible again,
people crossing the empty streets at midnight,
or during the rush hour
                        squeezed and overlapped by the living
before the lights change—
And this method must be used to think of them
or they disappear when you look
                        and no one is there.
This incident:
                        sitting with friends
in the chalet restaurant on top of Mount Royal
talking of a tree swaying back and forth in the wind,
leaving no silvery whip marks of its travelling self
                        or proof of passage
                                        we saying
"That tree will always be there."
Said in a commonplace tone it
doesn't sound exciting
                        but it is oh it is!

And something I've thought of every now and then:
how everything we do or say has an effect somewhere,
passes outward from itself in widening circles,
a sort of human magic by which
a word moves outside the nature of a word
as side effect of itself
                         the nature of a word being
that when it's been said it will always be said
—a recording exists in the main deep of sound.
And I think if there was a god somewhere
                    he'd be damn jealous.
It's a morbid idea perhaps,
if you don't think it's ridiculous:
so many line drawings of dead men,
so many white trails on downtown streets—
But I don't care much if it is for
it exalts me to think of those people
passing by tonight in the room where I sit writing,
on the roads that I will walk tomorrow
in the echoing rooms of yesterday—
And I think of the first space ship leaving earth,
going where men have never loved women,
                    or lived and died there
                    in the marginless emptiness
until the pale death angel of earth
                    comes for us on the star ships—